IN FOCUS: NATIVE AMERICANS

UTE
HISTORY AND CULTURE

MARK STEWART

Published in 2026 by Cavendish Square Publishing, LLC
2544 Clinton Street, Buffalo, NY 14224

Copyright © 2026 by Cavendish Square Publishing, LLC

No part of this publication may be reproduced, stored in a retrieval system, or transmitted in any form or by any means—electronic, mechanical, photocopying, recording, or otherwise—without the prior permission of the copyright owner. Request for permission should be addressed to Permissions, Cavendish Square Publishing, 2544 Clinton Street, Buffalo, NY 14224. Tel (877) 980-4450; fax (877) 980-4454.

Website: cavendishsq.com

This publication represents the opinions and views of the author based on his or her personal experience, knowledge, and research. The information in this book serves as a general guide only. The author and publisher have used their best efforts in preparing this book and disclaim liability rising directly or indirectly from the use and application of this book.

Portions of this work were originally authored by Lorraine Harrison and published as *Ute* (Spotlight on Native Americans). All new material this edition authored by Mark Stewart.

The website addresses (URLs) included in this book were valid at the time of going to press. However, it is possible that contents or addresses may have changed since the publication of this book. No responsibility for any such changes can be accepted by either the author or the publisher.

Publisher: Katie Kawa
Book Design: Lisa Miley

Portions of this work were reviewed by: Donald A. Grinde, Jr., Professor of Transnational/American Studies at the State University of New York at Buffalo.

Photo Credits: Don Fink/Shutterstock.com (4); Andrew J. Russell (5*); J.W. Powell & A.H. Thompson (6 top*); DEA/L. Romano/De Agostini/Getty Images (6 bottom); Wainwright Carsell/Author's Collection (7); William Armitage (9*); Bureau of American Ethnology (10*, 16*); Solomon Nunes Carvalho (11*); Charles Weitfle (12*); F.M. Steele/Library of Congress (13*); Brady-Handy Photograph Collection/Library of Congress (15*); Detroit Publishing Co. (17*); Rose and Hopkins (18*); Trees.com (19); Michael Buckner/Getty Images Entertainment/Getty Images (20); George Frey/AFP/Getty Images (21); Herschel Freeman Agency)22); Author's Collection (23, 29); Library of Congress (24*); David W. Hamilton/The Image Bank/Getty Images (25); Bernard Friel/Education Images/Universal Images Group via Getty Images (26-27); Chris Gardner/Getty Images (28).

Cover images (clockwise from top): Andrew J. Russell*; Chris Gardner/Getty Images; National Archives*; W.H. Jackson & Co.*; Author's Collection; Detroit Publishing Co.*.

*These images are in the public domain

Cataloging-in-Publication Data
Names: Stewart, Mark, 1960 July 7-.
Title: Ute history and culture / Mark Stewart.
Description: Buffalo, NY : Cavendish Square Publishing, 2026. | Series: In focus: Native Americans | Includes glossary and index.
Identifiers: ISBN 9781502674883 (pbk.) | ISBN 9781502674890 (library bound) | ISBN 9781502674906 (ebook)
Subjects: LCSH: Ute Indians--Juvenile literature. | Ute Indians--Social life and customs--Juvenile literature. | Indigenous peoples--Social life and customs--Juvenile literature.
Classification: LCC E99.U8 S94 2026 | DDC 979.004'974576--dc23

CPSIA compliance information: Batch #CS26CSQ: For further information contact Cavendish Square Publishing LLC at 1-877-980-4450.
Printed in the United States of America

CONTENTS

I AM THE LAND 4

FIRST CONTACT 8

I AM A WARRIOR 10

A NEW REALITY 14

BEING UTE 16

SOMETHING SACRED 20

PAST, PRESENT, FUTURE 24

GLOSSARY AND FURTHER READING 30

ABOUT THE AUTHOR 31

INDEX 32

ABOUT OUR GLOSSARY
In this book, there may be several words or terms you are reading for the first time, or words that are familiar but used in an unusual way. All of these words appear in **bold type** throughout the book and are defined on page 30.

I AM THE LAND

The Colorado Plateau is a vast, high desert region of the southwestern United States on the western side of the Rocky Mountains. It covers the "four corners," where Arizona, New Mexico, Colorado, and Utah meet—and includes Grand Canyon National Park and Zion National Park. For thousands of years, this area was home to the Capote, Grand River, Mouache, Tabaguache, Uintah, Weeminuche, and Yampa people. They are the original

Ute horsemen pose for the camera with mountains rising behind them. Long before acquiring horses in the 1700s, the Ute people moved easily between different ecosystems.

seven Ute tribes. The Utes moved their villages around these lands with the changing seasons, hunting and trapping game and fishing the streams and rivers that cut through their territory.

The Utes believed in living in harmony with the land around them. When they hunted, they used every part of the animal, so nothing went to waste. They were masters of their different **ecosystems**—expert trackers of large game in the mountains and deeply knowledgeable

◀ Ute Canyon in Colorado is typical of the landscape inhabited by the Ute people and their ancestors for thousands of years.

◀ This photo shows a Ute family in the 1870s.

about the plants and trees surrounding them. They also understood the importance of allowing the environment of favorite areas time to recover before returning. The Utes also did a limited amount of farming.

For many centuries, the rhythm of life for a Ute band was dictated by the amount of time it took to walk from one place to another. That changed with the introduction

of the horse to their culture after Spanish settlers arrived. The Utes bred and trained their horses to enable them to hunt and engage with their enemies over longer distances, stretching the boundaries of their world. Horses enabled them to raise cattle and sheep. The Utes also sold horses to their northern neighbors.

Today, the Ute people live mainly in Utah and Colorado, divided into three groups. The Northern Ute tribe, which is sometimes called the Ute tribe, lives mainly on a reservation in northeastern Utah. The Southern Ute tribe lives on a reservation in southwestern Colorado. A third and smaller group called the Ute Mountain tribe lives on a reservation in southwestern Colorado, southeastern Utah, and northern New Mexico.

The Utes became so good at hunting bison on horseback that, by the 1820s, the animals had all but disappeared from large portions of their territory.

◀ Ute territory in the "four corners" region features spectacular geological formations.

FIRST CONTACT

The Utes lived at the extreme reaches of the territory claimed by Spain in the 1500s and 1600s. As a result, they were not pressured to **convert** to Christianity (as other tribes were) or otherwise alter their way of life. Also, the Utes benefitted greatly from the horses they acquired from Spanish settlers. In time, however, increased contact with Europeans—both Spanish settlers and pioneers from the east—proved harmful. The Utes did not have immunity to the diseases they carried, such as **smallpox**. In some instances, tribe members were captured and enslaved.

The greatest challenge to Ute culture came in the 1840s with the arrival of the Mormons, a religious group fleeing persecution for their beliefs. The Mormons began moving onto Ute lands hoping to establish a place where they could live beyond the reach of the United States government. The place they chose was the Provo Valley,

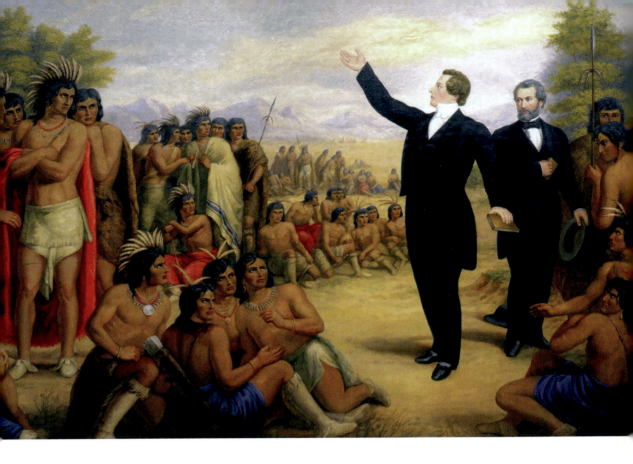

▲
This painting shows Mormon leader Brigham Young interacting with Northern Ute men. Young hoped their people would live in peace.

home of the Northern Utes. This set the stage for a series of brutal conflicts between the Mormons, the Utes, and the U.S. government, which had acquired the land from Mexico in 1848 and created the Utah Territory in 1850.

I AM A WARRIOR

The warrior tradition was strong among the Utes. Their culture embraced the idea of a "death-for-a-death," which was shared among people who spoke the **Numic** language, including the Paiutes and Shoshones. Every member of a Ute band, including women and children, was willing and capable of defending themselves if their village came under attack.

A Ute warrior was skilled with a bow and arrow and spear, as well as a throwing stick. All three were also used in hunting. A throwing stick resembled a small war club. Ute warriors also carried shields into battle. The Utes were the first tribe in the region to acquire horses. For many years, they were able to attack settlements of Apaches, Pueblos, and other groups

◀ This photo shows a Ute warrior identified as "Billy."

◀ Chief Walkara was an influential chief who made peace with the Mormons.

with little risk of **reprisal**. Their skill on horseback, developed over two centuries, gave them an edge in almost every confrontation, as did their intimate knowledge of their rugged environment.

If Ute warriors took prisoners, they were not above selling or trading them. This practice, though acceptable among many Native American cultures, created a **rift** with the Mormons, who did not support slavery on religious grounds and made attempts to prevent the Utes from engaging in this business. Initially, Mormon settlers hoped to enjoy peaceful relations by convincing their Ute "neighbors" that adopting an agricultural lifestyle was better than constantly moving in a search for food. In some cases, this worked.

However, the Northern Utes in particular were unwilling to abandon their traditions. The Mormon

stronghold of Salt Lake City grew to more than 10,000 people in the 1860s, making peaceful **coexistence** impossible. As more Utes were pushed off their lands, they began raiding Mormon settlements. Mormon leader Brigham Young urged his followers to be tolerant, believing that Native Americans could be converted to his faith.

Eventually violence erupted in 1853. It took a negotiation between Young and a Ute chief named Walkara to end the fighting. Walkara was a living legend among his people—a brave warrior and skilled negotiator who spoke English, Spanish, and several Native languages. An uneasy peace between the Mormons and Utes followed the series of skirmishes called the Walker War.

Ute warriors were particularly effective raiders. If their goal was to steal horses, they rarely came away empty-handed. If their aim was to exact revenge or "send a message," they could be unspeakably brutal.

◀ Three Ute warriors pose for a photo in 1850. The Ute people were feared and respected for their fighting skills.

A NEW REALITY

In 1849, the Utes signed a treaty that recognized the power of the United States government over them and allowed settlers to travel freely through their lands. Many people who arrived in Ute territory decided this was as far as they would go. They built **homesteads** and farms there, believing that the treaty gave them this right, and that they were now owners of Ute land. In 1859, gold was discovered in Colorado and more people flooded into Ute territory, also claiming land as their own.

Overwhelmed and outgunned, the Utes eventually agreed to move from their ancestral homes—not by choice, but as a means of survival—and settle on reservations. In 1864, the Northern Utes left their beloved Provo Valley and relocated to the Uintah Reservation, more than 100 miles (160 km) to the east. It later merged with another reservation to form the Uintah and Ouray Indian Reservation. In 1868, the Southern Utes began relocating to a large reservation in western Colorado.

Chief Ouray and his wife, Chipeta, posed for a series of portraits during their visit to Washington, D.C.

However, its size was greatly **diminished** after gold and silver were found on reservation lands.

The Ouray Reservation, which joined with the Uintah Reservation in 1886, was named after a Ute leader named Chief Ouray. He was responsible for negotiating many treaties with the federal government on behalf of the Ute people. In 1868, he traveled to Washington, D.C. and was recognized as the head chief of his people by the federal government.

BEING UTE

As a **nomadic** people, the Utes needed shelter that could be constructed upon their arrival in a particular area and then packed up and taken with them when it was time to move. They favored hide-covered tipis (tepees), which were easily transportable. They also built wickiups, dome-shaped huts made from **saplings** and covered with bark, as well as open structures that provided shade during the summer months, called ramadas.

Prior to the introduction of horses, the size of Ute encampments tended to be small, with individuals moving from band to band. As horses became a part of the tribal culture, bands grew in size and chose chiefs

◀ This hide painting offers an early glimpse of a Ute ceremony.

This 1885 photo shows the family of Sevaro, a Southern Ute chief. The two cradle boards used for carrying babies were typically gifts to a mother from other women in the family.

to lead them. Traditional Ute clothing was made from the hides of animals that were hunted or trapped. These included elk, deer, and bison hides, often with mink or rabbit fur for insulation.

Although the Utes were **shrewd** traders, the vast majority of the tools, weapons, and everyday items they used were fashioned from what was available to them courtesy of the natural world. Before iron became available, their knife blades and arrowheads were made from flint, and they continued to use stone and bone in their everyday toolmaking. Sheep and bison horn was used for a variety of purposes. Their bows came from the forests that dotted the Colorado Plateau and were typically made of cedar or chokecherry.

During the spring, Utes participated in a religious ceremony known as the Bear Dance. It is one of the oldest ceremonies practiced by the Ute people, whose mythology holds that they are close descendants of the

bear. The Bear Dance dates back to a time when survival through the winter was not assured. It is a four-day ceremony that celebrates life, and also recognizes deaths, births, and marriages. It is also a "ladies' choice" dance, with women in charge of picking their partners.

Gender roles have changed with the times, but traditionally women and girls ran the households in Ute bands. They were responsible for gathering and preparing plants for food and medicine. They did much of the cooking, made and repaired various garments, and produced baskets and pottery. Fishing and planting were often shared duties, while hunting, trading, and fighting was left to the men. Although women rarely held political power, they could be—and often were—**revered** tribal leaders.

Chokecherry was an important plant for the Utes. In addition to its use as bow-making material, its fruit was an ingredient in pemmican, a mixture of dried meat and berries that could be stored for long periods of time. Chokecherry's inner bark was used for a wide range of medicines.

◀ Women in Ute culture were responsible for a wide range of household duties. Their deep knowledge of local plants also made them expert healers.

SOMETHING SACRED

The most important ceremony for the Ute people was (and still is) the Sun Dance, which takes place every year in the middle of the summer. This ceremony is also known as "standing thirsty" because it involves the participants going without food and water for four days. During the Sun Dance, male Utes—who are called to participate through a spiritual vision—dance in order to obtain spiritual "medicine" powers.

Dance allows the Ute people to share their culture with the world outside their reservations. Raoul Trujillo is a dancer and **choreographer** of both Ute and Apache descent. He was the co-founder and first choreographer of the American Indian Dance Theater,

◀ Raoul Trujillo, a dancer, choreographer, and actor, has portrayed many memorable Native American characters on screen.

Grant Byron performs a traditional Ute dance for visitors to the 2002 Winter Olympics, in Salt Lake City, Utah. The tribe often uses sporting events to promote its cultural heritage.

as well as an actor who has appeared in more than 100 movies and televisions shows.

Joseph Rael, a Ute spiritual leader and writer, created new dances to help Utes and others around the world connect to their spirituality. He turned his visions into books, as well, including *Being and Vibration: Entering the New World* and an autobiography, *House*

R. Carlos Nakai is considered a master of the Native American flute. He has recorded more than 50 albums.

of *Shattering Light: Life as an American Indian Mystic*. Rael is also a painter whose works have been displayed in **galleries** throughout the western United States.

Where there is dance there is music, and this tradition is strong in Ute culture. Aaron White, a member of the Northern Ute and Diné (Navajo) tribes, is a master of the Native American flute who founded the group Burning Sky. Burning Sky combined Native American flute with **acoustic guitar** and drums, earning a **Grammy**

Award nomination in 2003. White believes music is medicine that can heal and mend the spirit. "All of us carry the gift of music in our heart and soul," he says. "May we always share these gifts with gratitude and warming hearts."

One of the artists who inspired White was R. Carlos Nakai, another master of the Native American flute, who is of Ute-Navajo heritage. Trained in **music theory** as a young man, he was handed a cedar flute in the 1980s and challenged to make music. The result was more than 50 albums and worldwide fame.

The language spoken by the Ute people is Numic, which is a branch of the Uto-Aztecan family. Uto-Aztecan is spoken by Native people from Nicaragua in the south to Idaho in the north. Numic is a language common to tribes from the Great Basin—between the Sierra Nevada and Rocky Mountains—and in parts of the southern Great Plains, too. Experts believe it is at least 2,000 years old. Although **dialects** differ from region to region, the Utes were able to communicate with other large tribes, including the Comanches, Paiutes, and Shoshones. For example, words for mountain (*kaipa*), bison (*kuttsu*), and hunt (*hoa*) sound nearly identical among the Numic-speaking tribes.

PAST, PRESENT, FUTURE

The promise of safety, which convinced Utes that reservation life was their best option, came at a high price. Hunger and disease were common. Tribal culture began to **erode**. The Utes were expected to speak English, abandon centuries-old belief systems, and convert to Christianity. While many Utes did convert, they also held on to some of the most sacred aspects of their traditional religion.

The Southern Ute Indian Reservation, located on Colorado's southern border (with New Mexico), is home to more than 12,000 people. The reservation's economy includes the **extraction** of natural resources

◀ As this 1906 photo of a Ute bridegroom shows, the tribe held on to important traditions after being relocated to reservations.

Preserving Ute culture and traditions is part of the relationship between parents and children.

with minimal disturbance to the environment, and the operation of the Sky Ute Casino Resort, a popular tourism destination and a place for business meetings and conventions. Many Southern Ute residents own or work for businesses outside of the reservation.

The Uintah and Ouray Indian Reservation is home to more than 25,000 people. At more than 4 million acres (1.6 million ha) in area, it is the second-largest reservation in the country. However, only about a quarter is tribal land. This is because, from 1905 to 1934, non-Ute people and businesses were allowed to buy land within its boundaries. As a result, there is an ongoing dispute between the Utes and the state of Utah over who has legal **jurisdiction** over tribal members.

The Ute Mountain Ute Indian Reservation is located in the four corners region. More than 1,200 people live on the reservation, which covers land in Colorado, New Mexico, and Utah. It is a very popular

This statue at the Northern Ute Veterans ▶ Memorial in Ballard, Utah, honors the tribe as the first people of the land.

destination for visitors interested in experiencing and learning about Ute history. Ute Mountain Tribal Park features archaeological sites, cliff dwellings, wall paintings, and **petroglyphs** that preserve ancestral Ute and Puebloan cultures. The tribal park has been kept as a primitive area to protect its beauty and importance, and tourists may only visit with a trained Ute guide.

Many people coming to the area stay in the Ute Mountain Casino Hotel, which opened in the 1990s. It features a restaurant that serves traditional foods eaten by the Ute people.

There is no mystery concerning the origin of the name of the 45th state, Utah. It was inspired by the Ute tribe. But where does the name "Ute" come from? It was commonly believed that it meant "people of the mountains." However, as the state's 100th anniversary celebration approached, no one seemed able to agree on its origin. Tribe members are quick to point out that no such word exists in their language. Utes call themselves *Noochee*, which means "the people." The name of the tribe has existed for centuries and was probably coined by Spanish settlers, who called them *Yutas*.

◀ A Ute dancer performs at halftime of a college football game between the University of California and University of Utah—whose sports teams are called the Utes. The tribe gave the school permission to use the name.

GLOSSARY AND FURTHER READING

GLOSSARY

Acoustic Guitar—A guitar that does not need an electronic amplifier.

Choreographer—A person who creates the steps and movements for a dance performance.

Coexistence—Living with others at the same time in the same place.

Convert—Accept a new religion.

Dialects—Slightly different forms of a language.

Diminished—Made lesser or smaller.

Ecosystems— Groups of living and non-living things that create nutrients and energy within various areas.

Erode—Slowly wear away.

Extraction—The action of removing something, including oil or minerals.

Galleries—Businesses that exhibit and promote the work of artists.

Grammy Award—A recognition of high achievement in music.

Homesteads—Properties that include a house as well as outbuildings, such as stables or a barn.

Jurisdiction—The power to make judgments and legal decisions.

Music Theory—The study of the basics for creating and understanding music.

Nomadic—Moving from place to place.

Numic—A family of Indigenous languages spoken by people from Central America to Canada.

Petroglyphs—Prehistoric rock carvings.

Reprisal—An act of retaliation.

Revered—Deeply respected and admired.

Rift—A break in friendly relations.

Saplings—Young, flexible trees.

Shrewd—Having sharp powers of judgment.

Smallpox—A virus brought to the Americas by Europeans, for which Indigenous people had no natural immunity. By the mid-1800s, more than 75 percent of Native Americans may have died of the disease.

BOOKS

Krupat, Arnold. *Boarding School Voices: Carlisle Indian School Students Speak*. Lincoln, NE: University of Nebraska Press, 2021.

Rossiter, Brienna. *The Trail of Tears*. Mendota Heights, MN: North Star Editions, 2025.

Tyler, Ron. *Native Americans: The Complete Plates of McKenney, Catlin, and Bodmer*. Cologne, Germany: Taschen America, 2024.

Various Authors. *My Life: Growing Up Native in America*. New York, NY: MTV Books/Simon & Schuster Children's Publishing, 2024.

ABOUT THE AUTHOR

MARK STEWART has written more than 150 non-fiction books for educational publishers, covering history, sports, and popular culture. His family tree tells a complex story common to many Americans. Mark's ancestors include some of the first European colonists, as well as the Indigenous people with whom early settlers interacted. Some faced off on the field of battle while others fought side-by-side. His 10th great-grandfather was **Myles Standish**, an officer on the *Mayflower*, while his ninth great-grandmother was **Singing Bird Corbison**, who was described as a "Shawnee woman" but who was probably from the **Wampanoag** tribe. The Wampanoag people saved Standish and his fellow **Pilgrims** from starvation during the winter of 1620–21, forming the basis for the story of Thanksgiving. The descendants of Corbison and Standish blended into a single family in 1789, and then headed west in search of opportunity. This brought Mark's ancestors into direct conflict with Native people along the frontier in the 1700s and 1800s. Mark's sixth great-grandmother recalled frantically casting bullets for her husband as they defended their small Kentucky fort from an attack. Another served under 23-year-old **Abraham Lincoln** in the Illinois Militia during the Black Hawk War of 1832. Mark's more recent ancestors chose to fight their battles with words—as writers and editors of books, newspapers, and magazines. In 2007, he authored a history of the **Indian Removal Act of 1830** and the infamous **Trail of Tears**.

INDEX

A

American Indian Dance Theater 20
Apache 10, 20

B

Bear Dance 18, 19
Billy, a Ute Warrior 10
Burning Sky 22
Byron, Grant 21

C

Chipeta 15
Chokecherry 19
Comanche 23

G

Grand Canyon National Park 4

N

Nakai, N. Carlos 21, 22
Navajo 22
Northern Ute Veterans Memorial . 26, 27
Numic 10

O

Ouray 15

P

Paiute 10, 23
Pueblo 10

R

Rael, Joseph 21, 22

S

Shoshone 10, 23
Sun Dance 20

T

Trujillo, Raoul 20

U

Ute Mountain Tribal Park 29
Uto-Aztecan 23

W

Walkara 11, 13
Walker War 13
White, Aaron 22, 23

Y

Young, Brigham 9

Z

Zion National Park 4